THE DECEMBER MAN

(L'homme de décembre)

The December Man

(L'homme de décembre)

Colleen Murphy

Playwrights Canada Press
Toronto • Canada

The December Man (L'homme de décembre) © 2007 Colleen Murphy
The moral rights of the author are asserted.

Playwrights Canada Press
The Canadian Drama Publisher
215 Spadina Avenue, Suite 230, Toronto, Ontario CANADA M5T 2C7
416-703-0013 fax 416-408-3402
orders@playwrightscanada.com • www.playwrightscanada.com

Financial support provided by the taxpayers of Canada and Ontario through the Canada Council for the Arts and the Department of Canadian Heritage through the Book Publishing Industry Development Programme, and the Ontario Arts Council.

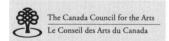 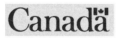

Front cover photo: Eagle Claw Thom. Cover design: JLArt.
Production Editor: Michael Petrasek

Library and Archives Canada Cataloguing in Publication

Murphy, Colleen, 1954-
    The December man = L'homme de décembre / Colleen Murphy.

A play, with text in English only.
ISBN 978-0-88754-595-5

    1. Montréal École Polytechnique Women Students Massacre, Montréal, Québec, 1989--Drama. I. Title. II. Title: Homme de décembre.

PS8576.U615D42 2007   C812'.54   C2007-902676-1

First edition: May 2007.
Printed and bound by Canadian Printco at Scarborough, Canada.

for Maureen Labonté

"Structural engineering is the backbone that provides strength and life to a load bearing structure"
—Engineering Textbook

"One cannot always be a hero, but one can always be a human."
—Johann Wolfgang von Goethe

The December Man (L'homme de décembre) received its world premiere as part of the Enbridge playRites Festival of New Canadian Plays 2007, at Alberta Theatre Projects, Calgary, Alberta, with the following company:

KATHLEEN Nancy Beatty
BENOÎT Brian Dooley
JEAN Rylan Wilkie

Directed by Bob White
Set Design by Scott Reid
Costume Design by Jenifer Darbellay
Composer/Sound Design by Kevin McGugan
Production Dramaturge: Vicki Stroich
Production Stage Manager: Dianne Goodman

Acknowledgements

The playwright thanks Maureen Labonté and Bob White, and acknowledges the support of the Ontario Arts Council Theatre Creators' Reserve, and the assistance of the 2006 Banff Playwrights Colony—a partnership between the Canada Council for the Arts, the Banff Centre and Alberta Theatre Projects.

Characters

JEAN Émile Fournier, 22
KATHLEEN Fournier (Kate), 62, Jean's mother
BENOÎT Fournier, 59, Jean's father

All eight scenes take place in the Fournier's living room. The action travels backwards in time, beginning March 1992 and ending December 1989.

Author's Notes

This is a work of imagination. My intention is not to exploit the events that took place on 6 December 1989 in the École Polytechnique where fourteen women were murdered, or to feed off the pain of families and friends who have been devastated, but to use the public event as a point of departure. While drawing on some facts from the historical record I have made no attempt to give a factual account of the event. I have altered and embellished reality and extended imaginary characters into real space and time. Any resemblance to real people is entirely coincidental.

Actual television newscasts that were broadcast on the evening of 6 December 1989 are not to be used. Each production must record the text on pages 57 to 59. Atmospheric sounds such as ambulance sirens and background voices may be added to make the recording more urgent.

No music is to be played before, during, or after the play.

Scene One

"...a happy little boy who always tried his best."

March 1992.

In this very modest living room, a matching couch and chair face out to the audience and a television faces in. Behind the couch are open drapes and behind those, heavy sheers. Bright, blinding sunlight pours in through the sheers. Side tables flank the couch on either side and a low coffee table rests in front. A phone sits on one of the side tables and a knitting basket is tucked under the coffee table. A Lazee-Boy is positioned to get the best view of the television. A large framed picture—an aerial photograph of Île St. Helene and Île Notre-Dame with "expo 67" written across the bottom—graces one wall while a framed high school graduation picture of a young man graces another, and a crucifix, another. On Stage Right (SR) is an entrance that leads to the kitchen, the basement, and the back door. On Stage Left (SL) is an entrance that leads off to the front door and down a hall towards the bedrooms. Everything in this room is neat and polished. There are throw rugs over the carpets, covers on the couch and chair, doilies under the lamp and on the back of the couch and Lazee-Boy.

A structure of what may have originally been a model of a highrise, sits on a piece of Plexiglas that is perched on a small table that stands in one corner. The structure is bottom-heavy, dusty, and held together with masking tape.

BENOÎT, dressed in his only suit, wanders into the living room and stands in front of the television. Childhood polio resulted in a slight limp. Absently he watches the screen as if waiting for something to happen... but the television is off. He seems uncomfortable in his freshly polished shoes and pressed white shirt, the collar of which is undone. He clutches a tie in one hand.

KATHLEEN enters from SL carrying a sealed envelope. She is dressed in a green dress, matching top and heels. Her hair is neatly done. She lays the envelope on the coffee table.

BENOÎT Green suits you.

KATE I bought it 'specially for his graduation.

> *BENOÎT nearly breaks into tears… but manages to hold back.*

Want help with that?

BENOÎT Yep. Don't get enough practice tying a tie, that's for sure.

> *She ties his tie…*

Okay, *pas trop serré.*

> *…then she finishes. Neither one knows what to do next.*

KATE We better sit down…

BENOÎT Yep.

> *They both sit on the couch. BENOÎT pulls up the knees of his pants.*

KATE How long do you think it'll take?

BENOÎT Not long—I turned it up full blast.

> *They wait… awkward, uncertain.*

KATE I saw a crocus this morning… out in the backyard near the fence.

BENOÎT That's early. They don't usually come up 'til April.

KATE A purple one… peeking up from under the snow. Guess winter's over.

BENOÎT Yep.

> *Silence.*

I'm suddenly hungry.

KATE Well I'm not getting up to cook anything now. Not even going to get you a glass of water, nothing. Kitchen's spotless and it's staying that way. No one's gonna accuse Kathleen Fournier of leaving a mess behind.

BENOÎT   The front door unlocked?

KATE   It's unlocked, Benoît.

BENOÎT   Check the towels?

KATE   They're all in place, good and snug.

BENOÎT   You put one down in front of the back door?

KATE   (*nods*) And the basement door.

BENOÎT   I'll double-check.

BENOÎT gets up and exits SR.

KATE   I checked everything twice.

A sound is heard coming from the kitchen.

Don't start pulling stuff out of the fridge.

BENOÎT   (*off*) Just getting a drink.

He enters with glass of whiskey and all but gulps it down.

KATE   Save me a sip.

BENOÎT   Finish it off.

She does so then hands him the glass.

KATE   Wash it and put it away.

BENOÎT exits SR.

Silence.

Are you washing that glass?

The sound of running water is heard for a second then BENOÎT re-enters—carrying a bottle of whiskey.

BENOÎT   I worry about the house exploding.

KATE   Nothing's gonna explode unless you light a cigarette.

BENOÎT   A match would speed things up, that's for sure.

KATE   Now someone's gonna find that empty bottle and think I—

BENOÎT   You told me to wash the glass—

KATE   Sit down—you're making me nervous.

> *BENOÎT sits back down on the couch.*

Should we turn off the lights?

BENOÎT   No. People will think we're not home.

KATE   Well, we're not gonna be home.

BENOÎT   We'll be home—we just won't know it.

KATE   We'll be in Heaven.

BENOÎT   No comment.

KATE   Don't argue with me. We'll be in Heaven... with Jean.

BENOÎT   I'm not arguing, Kathleen, I'm just saying we won't know we're here. We won't know where the hell we are—nobody knows, eh?

> *Silence.*

KATE   Madeleine is dropping by in the morning on her way to work.

BENOÎT   She's gonna be upset.

KATE   I feel terrible doing this to her but no way I want bugs crawling all over me.

BENOÎT   Maggots.

KATE   Eh?

BENOÎT   The kind of bugs that come along—maggots.

KATE   I'll call her at work and remind her.

> *KATHLEEN gets up and dials the phone.*

BENOÎT   Hurry up.

KATE   *(into the phone)* Madeleine, don't forget—oh, sorry. I'll wait.

> *Restless, BENOÎT gets up, walks around then sits back down again.*

(into the phone) Madeleine, morning. Eh? I'm just reminding you about tomorrow morning, eh—I told you three times I gotta go to the Caisse Populaire to sign... something—no, at the main branch and listen, if I'm not at the window by eight you just come in, you walk right in... Madeleine, I just want to say... I know you're busy but I... I just wanna say you're the best sister in the world, cooking up so much food and always helping us out—okay bye.

KATHLEEN hangs up the phone.

Good thing I phoned—she forgot all about tomorrow—got a memory like a spaghetti strainer.

She sits back down on the couch then indicates the envelope.

Better make sure that's facing up so she sees her name.

BENOÎT turns over the envelope on the coffee table.

BENOÎT   You write down our bank account number?

KATE   Account, deed for the house, money for Father Bonnière, instructions for what's-his-face over at the cemetery—it's all there.

KATHLEEN leans this way and that way... then she flops forward.

BENOÎT   What are you doing?

She reaches over and pulls the coffee table closer to the couch.

KATE   If you fall over, your head will rest on the table... or if I fall over.

BENOÎT   It's hard to fall over when you're sitting down.

KATE   I mean if you fall forward like this...

She illustrates by pitching forward and resting her head on the coffee table. It's a clumsy move.

BENOÎT   Is the door unlocked?

KATE   Yeah I said ten times—it's unlocked.

KATHLEEN gets up and exits SL.

BENOÎT   Where you going?

KATE   *(off)* ...be right back.

BENOÎT   Hurry up...

She comes back in carrying a man's red winter parka.

Cold?

KATE   No, I just wanna hold onto something that belonged to him.

She sits back down on the couch.

BENOÎT   Hold onto me.

KATE   I got it on sale. Remember?

BENOÎT   Yep.

KATE   Simone and me found big pre-Christmas bargains at the Bay. I was worried Jean wouldn't wear something so colourful—he never liked calling attention to himself—but he surely loved this parka, eh?

Silence.

BENOÎT   Never in a million years did I think things would turn out like this.

KATE   Me either.

Silence.

Bothers me that it's a mortal sin.

BENOÎT   No comment.

KATE   No comment, no comment. You should be a politician.

BENOÎT   You know what should be a mortal sin—beating the crap outta little kids. There should be an 11ᵗʰ commandment—Honour thy Children.

KATE   God knew what was best and stopped at ten.

BENOÎT   You know what you can do with God.

KATE   You don't believe in God you're not gonna go to
            Heaven and see Jean.

BENOÎT   I believe what I believe. I believe you open a kid's
            mouth and pour hate down their throat they're gonna
            grow up hating everything—women, men, kids, even
            puppies.

            Silence.

KATE   You think Jean hated us?

BENOÎT   I'm not talking about Jean—I'm talking about what
            happened to that guy.

            Silence.

KATE   Maybe Jean hated us a little... but mostly he started
            hating himself, eh?

BENOÎT   ...maybe.

            She begins to breathe too fast.

KATE   Soon it'll be okay, Benoît. We're gonna go to Heaven
            and see him. He'll be waiting there... he's gonna be all
            dressed up because he knows we're coming.

BENOÎT   Calm down or you'll end up having a heart attack
            before we get this over with.

            Silence.

KATE   You remember how Doctor Picard kept saying, Mrs.
            Fournier, you're almost forty you might wanna think
            of adopting and I say no way, we're gonna wait
            a little longer thank you very much, so I started
            praying. I prayed all summer when Expo was on
            and everything was crazy.

BENOÎT   Yep—crazy time. Whole city went crazy.

KATE   Remember the night we went to La Ronde?

BENOÎT   Yep.

KATE   Neon lights flickering... rode on all the rides, the
            Gyrotron, the Monster—oh my God that Monster was
            wild—we were screaming our heads off, eh?

BENOÎT   You smell the gas?

>   *She sniffs.*

KATE   Next morning I threw up all over the floor and you said I was nuts going on those rides at my age. But it wasn't the rides made me sick, was it?

BENOÎT   Sure wasn't.

>   *Silence.*

>   I smell the gas.

KATE   ...I'm afraid.

BENOÎT   Hold my hand. Take a couple deep breaths.

>   *Silence... except for her deep breathing.*

KATE   What if we don't go anywhere?

BENOÎT   Maybe we won't, Kathleen... maybe we'll never see Jean in person again but it doesn't matter 'cause already I see him.

KATE   You do?

BENOÎT   Yep.

KATE   Where?

BENOÎT   When I close my eyes. For a long time I only saw what I saw in the basement that morning... then I remembered Jean once telling me how he'd close his eyes and see buildings inside his head and how he'd swivel them around just by thinking. So I started thinking about that day in December, musta been early 70s, a big snowstorm and you and me and Jean—he was about six—we all went out in the backyard and made a snowman... so I just swivelled the pictures around and put that one in front of that other one. Now every time I close my eyes I see Jean running around inside my head, laughing, shouting, his arms fulla snow... a happy little boy who always tried his best.

KATHLEEN closes her eyes. After a moment her head drops ever so slightly to one side, away from BENOÎT.

BENOÎT lifts his arm that is already beginning to feel heavy and he puts it around her.

For a few moments his eyes remain open...

Blackout.

Scene Two

"I cannot keep standing at that door."

December 1991.

KATHLEEN sits on the couch wearing a housedress and slippers. Her hair is uncombed. She knits like a robot—the long needles clicking like a clock. The living room is messy, the drapes tightly closed.

The structure is situated more prominently than in the previous scene and though still taped together, it is not dusty.

The front door is heard opening and closing, then the sound of stamping boots. BENOÎT enters from SL dragging a small pine tree. He wears an old parka over his work clothes—forest green shirt and pants washed so many times they shine. He is in his stocking feet.

BENOÎT This is the smallest Bernard had. Where you want it?

KATE Doesn't matter.

BENOÎT By the window?

KATE Anywhere.

BENOÎT You bring up the tree stand?

KATE No, not yet.

He leans the tree against the wall then exits SR.

(calls) Your supper's in the oven.

BENOÎT *(off)* I'll get it later.

KATE   I made Jean's favourite, fish sticks and fries—even made tartar sauce.

He enters sans jacket, a glass of whiskey in his hand.

BENOÎT   Whatcha knitting now?

KATE   Ten toques, ten sweaters, and ten pair of mittens to match.

BENOÎT   That's a lot of wool.

KATE   The Church women are paying for it—same as always. They got money those old gals. Don't know where they get it—no one goes to Church anymore.

BENOÎT sits down on the Lazee-Boy.

These hats got little pointy ears like a cat, see? *(holds up her knitting)* For the next batch I'm gonna use white wool to sew snowflake shapes on top of the toques, make them look like snowflakes landed on their heads—cute idea, eh?

BENOÎT absently turns on the television.

T.V.   *(female reporter's voice)* "And now the headlines: Today, exactly two years after what has become known as the Montreal Massacre, December 6th is officially declared a National Day of Remembrance"—

KATE   Turn that off!

BENOÎT   *(hurries to turn it off)* Tabarnac—

KATE   Turn that off right now—

BENOÎT   I didn't know it was gonna be on—

KATE   Don't you turn that TV on tonight—not for a second—not for one second!

BENOÎT   Okay, okay.

KATE   What are you—stupid?

BENOÎT   No I'm not stupid.

KATE   Then how come you didn't know that today is today?

BENOÎT   I know what today is.

KATE   You forgot.

BENOÎT   I didn't forget, Kathleen.

KATE   How could you forget?

BENOÎT   I didn't forget—I just don't think about it every second of my life—I go to work so I can bring home a friggin' paycheque. Maybe you should go back to work instead of hanging around the house all day knitting for free—

KATE   It's for the Christmas Charity Baskets at Our Lady of Fatima!

BENOÎT   *Crisse*—let the rich ladies knit for free. Get a job—you need to get out of the house.

KATE   Mrs. Jamison says I can have my old job back whenever I want.

BENOÎT   I thought she hired another woman.

KATE   Simone can't clean that big house all by herself—that new woman's just temporary. Mrs. Jamison said the job's mine when I feel like going back.

BENOÎT   I don't trust the rich and their pity.

KATE   She said she'd even pay me a bit more.

BENOÎT   What are you waiting for, eh?

KATE   I'll go back when I'm ready.

BENOÎT   Yeah, I hope it's some time this century.

BENOÎT exits SR...

KATE   Go bring up the tree stand and the decorations.

...BENOÎT enters with his glass refilled.

BENOÎT   I told you—no way I'm going down the basement.

KATE   Then that tree's just gonna lie there—bare like that.

BENOÎT   Didn't want a tree in the first place.

KATE	It's Christmas.
BENOÎT	So? No one's gonna look at it 'cept us. You want to stand it up and decorate it, you go down the basement and get the decorations yourself.
KATE	Madeleine can go down and get them. She's coming tomorrow to take me shopping.
BENOÎT	Shopping for what?
KATE	Your Christmas gift.
BENOÎT	I don't want a Christmas gift.
KATE	You need a new pair of work gloves.
BENOÎT	Save the money.
KATE	Your gloves are tore out in five places.
BENOÎT	I don't care.
KATE	You don't care about anything. At least I try—I help keep little children warm, little children who have no one—it's giving to others. What do you give, eh?
BENOÎT	I got nothing to give.

...BENOÎT gets up and exits SR.

KATE	You think I like sitting here knitting 'til my fingers swell up—no. I force myself—and I pray, I pray and go to Church—which is more than I can say for you.

BENOÎT enters with another glass of whisky.

BENOÎT	I go to church when I have to.
KATE	I saw what you did to your rosary, Benoît.
BENOÎT	Eh?
KATE	Your rosary.
BENOÎT	You bin snooping in my bureau—
KATE	I wasn't snooping—
BENOÎT	*Calisse—*

KATE   I was putting away your laundry and the crucifix was sticking out from under your shorts. When I went to tuck it back I saw that the rosary was busted to pieces. That's a sin, Benoît—purposely damaging a holy object is a mortal sin. That rosary was blessed by Cardinal Léger—you're gonna be in big trouble with the Church.

BENOÎT   I don't care.

BENOÎT exits SR with his empty glass...

KATE   You don't care about anything 'cept your whiskey and smokes and hockey games and the guys at work feeling sorry for you and not saying anything when you're drunk on the job!

...and re-enters with his glass full.

BENOÎT   Shut up—you just shut up! I care about Jean—he's all I care about!

KATE   *(throws down her knitting)* I hate them, I hate them and I want to hate her most of all but I can't hate any more... I just can't. I should stick a fork in my throat for saying this but I feel sorry for that Mrs. Lépine. I know how she musta felt when her son died and even though he deserved to die a thousand times she musta felt like I do now... prob'ly worse.

BENOÎT   No, no one feels worse than me.

KATE   I do.

BENOÎT   Okay, maybe you.

KATE   For sure I feel worse.

BENOÎT   No, we're equal. You and me we're a terrible kind of equal.

KATE   The mothers of those young women... how do they keep breathing? Honest to God, Benoît, how do they keep breathing...

Silence.

BENOÎT   We should move.

KATE   Eh?

BENOÎT   Sell the house. Move.

KATE   Move where?

BENOÎT   Smaller house, new neighbourhood. Move up to Chomedey—be closer to Madeleine.

KATE   I can't leave Jean's room behind.

BENOÎT   You never go into his room, never go down the basement—you sit here week after week like a lump— why stay? Let's sell the house and move far away.

KATE   Far away to where—Ontario?

BENOÎT   Maybe back to Gaspé.

KATE   There's nothing there 'cept your ma's old house—and how would I visit Jean everyday? He walked past that cemetery all the time—you think he sensed someday he'd be buried—

BENOÎT   Don't start getting morbid.

BENOÎT exits SR with his empty glass, and re-enters with his glass full.

KATE   Maybe he changed his mind, eh?

BENOÎT   Who?

KATE   Jean.

BENOÎT   What are you talking about?

KATE   At night when I'm lying awake I hear footsteps coming up the basement stairs… soft footsteps. You're usually asleep or passed right out—but I get up and go into the kitchen and stand in front of the basement door and pray. I pray that he undid the rope and got down off the chair, and that now he's on the other side of the door and wants me to open it. Remember that time Madeleine gave him those Sea Monkeys and he took them down to the basement, filled the laundry sink and I guess he stuck the spongy crap into the water and it started wiggling so he come running up the stairs yelling "Ma, Ma... they're alive, they're alive"... remember?

BENOÎT Barely.

KATE "They're alive, Ma, they're alive they're alive they're alive"—

BENOÎT Stoppit, Kate.

KATE Once you said Jean had tears on his face 'cause maybe he changed his mind at the last moment. Do you think he changed his mind? Please, Benoît... tell me he changed his mind and this is just a bad dream...

Silence.

BENOÎT No, Kathleen, he didn't change his mind.

KATHLEEN begins to weep. BENOÎT comforts her.

Shhh Kathleen... it's gonna be okay. You don't have to go back to work 'til you want. We still got some money left from that collection the guys at work took up. We'll be okay...

KATE No. I cannot... I cannot keep standing at that door.

Blackout.

Scene Three

"Look what you've all gone and done."

August 1991.

A little portable fan is going. It is a hot day. Bright light bleeds through the sheers.

Wearing a sleeveless blouse and an old skirt, her hair messy, KATHLEEN absently but furiously dusts the coffee table and television, but when she gets to the structure, she dusts it with great care. The structure, sleeker than in the previous scene, leans to one side as if the load it bears is too heavy, but it has not yet been broken so there is no tape on it. She looks at the dusting

> *rag in hand... then stops dusting and stares at it as if stuck on a thought.*
>
> *BENOÎT enters from SR. His shirtsleeves are rolled up.*

BENOÎT   What's for supper?

KATE   I don't know.

BENOÎT   Eh?

KATE   Madeleine brought over a couple casseroles.

BENOÎT   What kind?

KATE   I don't know—macaroni and cheese. Other one looks like meatloaf.

BENOÎT   Oh boy.

> *He goes out SR. After a moment he returns with a drink—whiskey—which he downs in one or two gulps.*

You're not gonna believe this, eh.

KATE   What?

BENOÎT   Nelsons are putting in air conditioning. Got a memo today—everyone just 'bout fainted from shock. Forty-seven years they're in business now, August 1991, they're finally gonna put in AC, eh *crisse—ça s'peut pas!*

KATE   Do that again...

BENOÎT   What again?

KATE   Walk over there and back.

BENOÎT   Why?

KATE   Just walk!

> *BENOÎT walks across the room... a little unsteady on his feet.*

Anyone can see your limp a mile away.

BENOÎT   It's worse when I'm tired and I'm tired 'cause I'm boiling to death.

KATE   Look at this...

BENOÎT   Eh?

KATE   *(holds up the rag)* You see what this is?

BENOÎT   Yeah.

KATE   What is it?

BENOÎT   A rag.

KATE   Sometimes you're stupid.

BENOÎT   Eh?

KATE   Sometimes you're stupider than a block of wood.

BENOÎT   Lay off.

KATE   This is a piece of his pyjamas, the ones with the bumblebees he got for his eighth birthday, see—1975 and we had a party right here in this room and that little girl from next door came—Patty something—she came over in a little frilly dress and brought Jean Play-Doh and we gave him these and a Lego thing and I wrapped up some quarters in wax paper and put them in the cake. You remember?

BENOÎT   I remember she swore a lot for a little kid.

KATE   She found two quarters in the cake and got so excited she vomited but we had fun.

          KATE exits SR.

BENOÎT   Where you going?

KATE   *(off)* Out to the garage to get a shovel.

BENOÎT   What for? Kathleen?

          KATHLEEN sticks her head back into the room.

KATE   Put your shoes back on—we're going over to the cemetery.

BENOÎT   You were just there this morning.

KATE   Not where Jean is—the other one.

BENOÎT Eh?

KATE Côte-des-Neiges.

BENOÎT Ah, come on Kathleen—now who's being stupid?

KATE You just shut up and go get me that shovel 'cause I'm gonna go dig up that son-of-a-bitch's grave, break his coffin open and bash his skull into powder—

BENOÎT You just settle down.

KATE *(holds up the cleaning rag)* This is all I got left—this, some toys, a few snapshots and that son-of-a-bitch-of-a-murdering killer he's resting in peace up there in that big fancy Catholic graveyard full of famous people, even a saint—Saint Marguerite d'Youville— a murderer's lying in the same ground as a certified saint and in the same ground as the first lady governor general and all kinds of famous poets, oh my God there's famous people lying all over that place—

BENOÎT Yeah, there lots of famous people up there 'cause it's beautiful and it's quiet and it's got pretty trees and scenery and people are always walking through it on Sunday afternoons and talking softly and admiring the headstones. Jean he loved that mountain—he shoulda been buried up there too!

KATE You think I'd let my son lay in the same ground as his killer?

BENOÎT That guy didn't kill Jean.

KATE Yes, he did—he murdered him.

BENOÎT You're crazy.

KATE He murdered him—and he murdered me and he murdered you!

BENOÎT Jean killed himself, Kate!

KATE I KNOW THAT!

BENOÎT Don't scream at me—you're the one cutting up his pyjamas for rags.

KATE   I did it a long time ago. I didn't know he was gonna—
if I knew what was gonna happen you think I'd cut up
his clothes, eh—you damned stupid fool!

BENOÎT   I told you to get help for him.

KATE   I tried but you were always saying "He's fine, Kate,
he's fine." How many times I tell you he needed to
talk to someone—how many times I tell you that?

BENOÎT   Then you shoulda picked up the phone and called
someone 'stead of buggin' him about marks—he
couldn't concentrate on friggin' marks!

KATE   Every time I said he should talk to someone you'd say,
"Karate lessons are giving him confidence." What
confidence? He couldn't walk through the door of that
school any more, could barely get on the Metro.
Jumping up and down like a Mexican jumping bean—
where'd it get him, eh, Dr. Benoît Fournier? He was
lost. I tried to find him but I didn't know where to
look—neither did you!

BENOÎT   Don't blame me—I never hurt Jean his whole life—
even when he accidentally stepped on that kitten we
bought him, I never raised my voice. Took him fishing,
tobogganing—he always talked to me about his
engineering and okay, most of the time I didn't know
what the hell he was talking about but I'd nod my
head 'cause I didn't want him to think I was dumb.
Twenty-three years I look after him then one morning
I go down the basement... oh boy oh boy, that's the
big problem, Kathleen. I can't wipe that picture off my
eyes. Every morning I wake up that picture's first
thing I see—that's if I actually close my eyes during
the night 'cause first thing I see when I close my eyes
at night is that same goddamn picture.

KATE   I saw him, too. After you took him down and laid him
on the floor.

BENOÎT   He had tears down the side of his face.

KATE   Eh?

BENOÎT They dried up by the time you got home but I seen them. I used to think maybe he changed his mind last minute but he didn't know what else to do 'cause we couldn't hear what he was saying to us.

KATE What was he saying?

BENOÎT He was saying, "Help me," and maybe if someone helped him he wouldn't be laying over there in that piece of shit Parc Commémoratif where they don't allow you to raise a stone—they make you put down a goddamn stupid flat cement block you can hardly see and grass grows over and people walk all over my son's head—

KATE It's eight blocks from here—I can walk over and visit him every single day.

BENOÎT Yeah, for you it's an hour a day, for Jean it's forever—he's gotta lie there with traffic rumbling by along the Côte-de-Liesse and six friggin' lanes on the Metropolitan and hundreds and hundreds of friggin' trucks, the goddamn noise must be rattling his bones apart—Jean's the one's gonna be powder pretty soon, thanks to you.

KATE Get out!

BENOÎT He's my son too, Kate!

KATE Oh yeah, oh yeah.

BENOÎT Just 'cause you and Madeleine and Father friggin' Bonnière never asked me my opinion 'bout burying Jean in that piece of shit—

KATE You were drunk the whole time we were making arrangements and you're drunk now—get out!

BENOÎT I'm going—and I'm gonna buy some smokes—buy a whole carton!

KATE Fine—go smoke yourself to death.

BENOÎT *Va chier!*

　　　　BENOÎT exits SR.

KATE   And don't come back.

BENOÎT   *(off)* Fuck you.

KATE   F you too.

> ...*KATHLEEN listens to the door opening then being slammed shut.*

Va Chier!

> *She blindly picks up the structure and smashes it and smashes it and smashes it some more. Then she stops...*

Look what you've done. Look what you've all gone and done...

> *Blackout.*

Scene Four

"Jean... did you fall asleep down there?"

April 1991.

The sound of a door closing is heard. After a moment JEAN enters from SR wearing a worn spring jacket over his clothes. His face is haggard. He turns on the television and flops down on the couch.

The structure stands abandoned in a corner and leans very much to one side.

Suddenly, JEAN gets to his feet and executes a few moves—a side kick (yoko geri kekomi) a front snap kick (mae gerie) and maybe a roundhouse (mawashi geri). He executes them well—graceful and lethal at the same time. Then, as quickly as he got to his feet, he slumps back down on the couch again and sits in the dark, the light from television cartoons flickering across his face.

KATHLEEN pops her head in from SL. She wears a housecoat over her nightgown and knitted slippers on her feet.

KATE   You're up early on a Saturday morning.

JEAN   Got in late.

KATE   What are you watching? Cartoons?

JEAN   Nothing...

     She opens the drapes. Dawn is breaking—a rainy day.

KATE   Want some breakfast?

JEAN   I'm not hungry.

KATE   When did you come in?

JEAN   Late.

KATE   How late is late?

JEAN   Around one.

KATE   Where were you?

JEAN   At a movie.

KATE   What movie?

JEAN   "Teenage Mutant Ninja Turtles 2."

KATE   Thought you saw it last week.

JEAN   Felt like seeing it again.

KATE   How many times you sit through it?

JEAN   Twice.

     KATE turns off the television.

KATE   You didn't get in 'til four.

JEAN   Ma, I keep telling you—don't wait up for me.

KATE   I didn't—just happened to look at the alarm clock when you came in.

JEAN   I sat out in the backyard for a couple hours. Moon was out... full moon. I was trying to envision a building... or a park.

KATE   A park?

He gets up, walks over to the structure and lifts it up.

JEAN   It's time to throw this in the garbage.

KATE   No, leave it there. You should have handed it in.

JEAN   It's not good enough—it's lopsided.

KATE   If you bend your head a little it looks straight.

JEAN   *Sensei* once said there were five rules to being happy: Free your heart from hatred. Free your mind from worries. Live simply. Give more. Expect less.

KATE   Well that guy he can say what he likes about being happy—for me being happy is knowing that every house I clean for bitches like Mrs. Jamison—pardon the language—but they pick away at me until I'm just bone, they gripe about this, howl about that, the smallest piece of dust, smudge on a crystal vase from Czechoslovakia—I gotta put my head inside their toilet bowl and lick it before they're satisfied it's clean. They look at me like I'm stupid, like I don't have a son who's at university studying to be an engineer, like I'm a ghost who floats though their big house licking their toilet bowls, dusting their expensive trinkets so they can pay me a hundred and fifty a week cash under the table. I get no benefits, no QPP, no UIC... maybe I get ten dollars in a Christmas card—no, Jean, for me being happy is knowing that in June I'm going to dress up in my new green dress and Benoît he's gonna be in his suit and we're gonna watch you walk up to the stage wearing a gown and cap—you're gonna be the first ever in my family since we come across—the first ever to go to university, first ever to graduate and I'm gonna borrow Madeleine's camera and take snaps then we're coming back here and have fancy cake and champagne and it's gonna be the happiest day in my life. So yes, you are gonna finish this and I'm gonna help you because you're going to get your degree—now let's straighten it up.

She touches the structure.

JEAN   Leave it alone, Ma.

KATE   Things might have gone better if you'd built a church.

JEAN   Eh?

KATE   If this had been a church—maybe things might have turned out better.

JEAN   Don't be stupid, Ma—

KATE   I'm not stupid!

JEAN   Sorry—

KATE   You don't ever call me stupid.

JEAN   I'm sorry. The assignment wasn't to build a church but design a skyscraper—Ma, don't touch!

KATE   Maybe if we put something under one side to help tip it back this way—

JEAN   Leave it alone—

KATE   We can fix it, Jean—

JEAN   IT CAN'T BE FIXED—IT CAN NEVER BE FIXED!

KATE   Shhhh—you'll wake your father.

JEAN   Even if I remodelled it, finished the calculations and handed it in, I won't get my degree—least not this year.

KATE   Why not?

        Silence.

JEAN   I haven't been going to class.

KATE   Eh?

JEAN   Haven't been attending classes.

KATE   You leave every morning with your lunch pail—what do you mean you're not attending classes.

JEAN   I didn't want you to freak out.

KATE   ...what are you doing all day?

JEAN   Go for walks.

KATE	...walks?
JEAN	I didn't want you to worry.
KATE	Going for walks all day—where?
JEAN	On the mountain.
KATE	Where on the mountain?
JEAN	Up around Beaver Lake and the Chalet, but mostly along the trails. The bare trees are beautiful. Snow's melting and streams of water are running and when the sun comes out everything sparkles. I apologize to them. I whisper to them, to the air... to their souls.
KATE	Whisper to who?
JEAN	The women.
KATE	Jean, what are you talking about?
JEAN	I take them on my walks—all of them, and point out interesting structures... show them shapes and buildings—the Biodome, Olympic Stadium, compositions of landscape in different kinds of light, or look beyond the city and point out the Laurentians in the distance. I was thinking of switching to Architecture so I can design a park... a park with fountains and gardens.

She takes a few deep breaths.

KATE	The doctor says I shouldn't get riled up but I don't understand you—you quit karate, wasted all that money—why?
JEAN	I'm sorry. I'll get something full-time and pay you and P'pa back. There's a new video store opening at Dècarie and MacDonald.
KATE	In a week you'll be 24—don't end up like your father—his family was poor 'cause they had no education.
JEAN	P'pa understands basic engineering.
KATE	He's only got grade five.
JEAN	He's smart. He always asks me questions.

KATE   I can see you sitting in a big fancy office, drawing diagrams.

JEAN   Ma, I'm sorry. I tried my best, but I couldn't keep going back into that building—the smell of blood, the sounds, and now when I build structures there's always people inside them... and I can't get them out.

KATE   Who?

JEAN   The people.

KATE   What people?

JEAN   They're running around inside my buildings... screaming.

KATE   What buildings... *(points to the structure)*...that one?

JEAN   No—the ones in my head. Sometimes I mentally take the roof off and tip the structure upside down to shake the people out... but they're stuck, they're stuck to the shear and they'll never let go because they can't... they're stuck, so am I—I'm stuck inside that building, Ma. I thought I ran out... but I didn't.

KATE   You haven't eaten since yesterday—running around to movies and up all night, no wonder things are shaking inside you—you need breakfast.

JEAN   I'm not hungry right now.

        JEAN wearily heads for the kitchen.

KATE   Where are you going?

JEAN   Down the basement.

KATE   No, you rest, or go have a nice hot shower. I'm gonna get dressed and go buy sausages—make you a big breakfast.

JEAN   I need to practise my moves.

KATE   Why? You quit karate, quit school, you skip Mass nearly every Sunday now—what are you gonna do— kick the air? Pretend you're a goddamn hero—who you gonna save down there, eh?

JEAN   I'm no hero, Ma—you know that.

KATE   I'm sorry, Jean, forgive me for saying such awful things. Forgive me.

              JEAN hugs his mother.

JEAN   I forgive you, Ma. It's not your fault it happened—it just happened, but now I have to look after them.

KATE   You have to look after yourself... and I have to look after you.

              BENOÎT enters from SL wearing pyjama bottoms.

BENOÎT   Who won the shouting match?

JEAN   Sorry, P'pa.

BENOÎT   C'mon, we gotta get going.

KATE   Where?

BENOÎT   Jean and me are going fishing over at Lac St. Louis. *(to JEAN)* Take maybe twenty minutes to get to Lachine, stop and get bait, eh—you almost ready?

JEAN   ...I don't feel like going fishing today.

BENOÎT   Why not? In this weather fish are gonna be jumping right out of the water.

KATE   Jean's tired.

JEAN   P'pa...?

BENOÎT   Eh?

              JEAN seems to want to say something to his father and for a moment they look at each other in expectation... then JEAN turns away and exits SR to go down to the basement.

KATE   *(lowers her voice)* Something's wrong with him. He's talking crazy, people stuck inside buildings that are stuck inside his head.

BENOÎT   He always sees stuff inside his head, no big deal.

KATE   Call Father Bonnière or Doctor Picard first thing
           Monday, and keep things extra normal today. Is there
           a hockey game tonight?

BENOÎT   Yep—Habs against the Sabres.

KATE   Ask Jean if he wants to watch the game with you.

BENOÎT   Why—he doesn't care about hockey.

KATE   Tell him it's a special game or something.

BENOÎT   It's special for sure—we win we're in the semi-finals.

KATE   I'll pop popcorn—make it a family evening, eh?

           KATE exits SL.

BENOÎT   Yeah okay, but... Kathleen... it's not normal.

KATE   *(off)* What?

BENOÎT   Sitting together eating popcorn and watching a
           game—we never did it his whole life. He'll think it's
           weird.

KATE   *(off)* You got a better idea?

BENOÎT   Yeah, don't do nothing. I'll talk to Father Bonnière
           tomorrow after Mass.

           She re-enters wearing a housedress.

KATE   I'm gonna go buy sausages. Put the coffee on.

BENOÎT   When did he get in last night?

KATE   Early this morning.

BENOÎT   Maybe he's got a girlfriend.

KATE   Oh, I hope so. A nice girl to go around with would
           cheer him up.

BENOÎT   Maybe after breakfast he'll be in the mood to go
           fishing.

           *KATHLEEN exits SR. A door is heard closing as she
           leaves.*

           (calls) Jean, I'm making coffee—you want some?

BENOÎT exits SR.

The sounds of BENOÎT making coffee, opening cup-boards, and pouring water...

(off, calls) Jean...

A clatter and minor curse as he gets the cups...

(off, calls) Jean? You fall asleep down there?

Silence.

(off) Jean...

Silence.

Blackout.

Scene Five

"Those people are permanently out of our lives."

December 1990.

The living room is dark... it's dark and cold outside. A decorated Christmas tree sits in one corner with an angel perched on top.

The structure stands in one corner still leaning noticeably to one side as if the load it bears is either imbalanced or too heavy.

The back door is heard opening and closing then the sound of stamping boots. KATHLEEN enters from SR wearing a worn out winter coat and a pair of knitted slippers on her feet. She turns on the lights, closes the drapes... then exits SR. After a moment she re-enters but this time without her coat. She plugs in a cord and the tree lights begin to twinkle, then she exits SL.

The back door is heard opening and closing again... again the sound of stamping boots.

BENOÎT   *(off)* Bonjour, ma belle.

KATE   *(off)* You buy the tinsel?

BENOÎT   *(off)* Yep. On sale. *Kistie, qui fais frette!*

> *KATHLEEN enters from SR carrying an envelope and
> a newspaper. She tosses the newspaper on the Lazee-Boy
> then opens the envelope and pulls out a letter... as she
> reads it her face tightens.*

> *After a moment BENOÎT enters from SR his face still
> red from the cold outside, knitted slippers on his feet,
> a box of tinsel in his hand and struggling with a large
> square of Plexiglas.*

Look what I brought Jean from work.

KATE   His mid-term marks are terrible... *(reads)* "Reinforced Concrete II... 51, Structural Analysis 49" and look... all the classes he missed.

> *BENOÎT sets down the Plexiglas and looks at the letter
> with her.*

BENOÎT   ...*Crisse*, that's a lot.

KATE   Why'd he miss that many?

BENOÎT   Maybe he was working on more projects.

KATE   I don't understand. He studied every day. I watched him—he studied like a maniac.

BENOÎT   Maybe the tests are getting harder.

KATE   That karate nonsense is affecting his schoolwork.

BENOÎT   It's helping him get his confidence back.

KATE   What's more important—getting confidence or getting a degree?

BENOÎT   He's gonna be fine, Kate.

KATE   You said that last spring but his June report was lousy—I don't understand. He's always had good marks. Maybe he's got into the dope or something.

BENOÎT   He's not into the dope.

> *The back door is heard opening and closing.
> KATHLEEN lowers her voice.*

KATE   I think he's into the dope, Benoît. Mrs. Jamison's son—
       son *and* daughter—I find bits of dope in their bureau
       drawers... and in their pockets.

BENOÎT   What kind of dope?

KATE   I don't know—pot.

BENOÎT   Jean doesn't smoke pot.

KATE   You see it all the time now... students spending
       money on pot, running around having fun while
       their parents starve to death.

BENOÎT   He's gonna be fine, Kate.

KATE   Your head's stuck in the sand like one of those big
       birds.

BENOÎT   Stop going at me—just stop!

KATE   Why's he skipping all these classes?

BENOÎT   I don't know—ask him.

       *BENOÎT sits down on the Lazee-Boy to escape into the
       paper.*

KATE   *(calls)* Jean...

JEAN   *(off)* ... coming.

KATE   *(calls)* Get in here right now!

BENOÎT   Take it easy, Kate.

JEAN   *(off)* Just a second...

       *JEAN enters wearing a new red parka and carrying his
       slippers.*

       It's freezing out there.

KATE   Were you at classes today?

JEAN   At least say hello before you jump down my throat.

KATE   Hello, Jean. Were you at classes today?

JEAN   Hi, Ma.

KATE   Were you?

JEAN   Yeah. This morning.

KATE   What about this afternoon?

JEAN   ...no.

KATE   (to BENOÎT) See, he skipped again.

BENOÎT Shouldn't skip classes, Jean.

JEAN   I was at the memorial.

KATE   Eh?

JEAN   At school.

KATE   Thought you said you weren't gonna go to it.

        Silence.

JEAN   Lots of people went, Ma. Lots of guys.

        BENOÎT exits SR into the kitchen.

KATE   Shouldn't have gone. Now you'll start getting
        nightmares again.

JEAN   It was important for us to be there.

        BENOÎT re-enters with a beer.

KATE   Jean, you've got to get over what happened, else your
        marks are gonna get worse and they can't get much
        worse than this.

        She hands him the letter. He glances at it...

JEAN   Shouldn't open mail that's addressed to me.

        ...then he hands the letter back to her.

        P'pa, could I have one of your beers?

BENOÎT Eh?

JEAN   Could I have a beer?

BENOÎT Want a beer?

JEAN   Yeah.

        BENOÎT exits SR.

KATE   Why'd you skip so many classes?

JEAN   ...don't know.

KATE   If you'd been really smart you'd have skipped classes this exact day last year and saved us all a lot of trouble.

JEAN   I'll do better next term, Ma. I promise.

> *Silence.*

KATE   What was it like?

JEAN   What?

KATE   The memorial.

> *BENOÎT re-enters with two beers. He hands one to JEAN.*

JEAN   It was sad. People were crying. (Thanks, P'pa.) School wasn't too happy about reporters hanging around. Someone said next year the school won't hold a service.

KATE   Best thing for everyone is to put the whole thing behind them.

JEAN   Some guys were talking... they said they'd heard that Lépine's mother used to be a nun. Weird, eh?

BENOÎT   Boy oh boy oh boy.

KATE   I don't want to hear any more about those people, they're getting crazier by the minute. If she'd stayed in the convent maybe none of this would've happened. You gotta wonder why she left the convent to marry a man who I heard beat her kids 'til they bled from their ears.

BENOÎT   Who told you that?

KATE   Madeleine heard it somewhere—too bad he didn't beat that kid to death before the kid left home.

BENOÎT   Okay, don't get crazy.

KATE   Now we find out he had a list of famous women he was gonna kill—had them lined up like bowling pins.

BENOÎT   Okay, okay enough!

JEAN exits SR.

KATE   *(to JEAN)* Where you going?

JEAN   Downstairs.

KATE   Come back here.

JEAN pokes his head into the room.

JEAN   I need to practise my moves.

KATE   No you don't.

JEAN   It helps me concentrate.

KATE   You concentrate on finishing your design project. It's gonna fall over if you don't fix it. How you gonna get an "A" when it's already a week overdue?

JEAN   I don't feel like it right now.

BENOÎT   Maybe you feel like getting up at six every morning and going to Nelson's so you can have the thrill of spending eight hours making radar drives and worm screw jacks and friggin' gear couplings, eh? You wanna trade places?

JEAN   No, P'pa.

BENOÎT   Your ma worries about you all the time—she drives me nuts worrying, so you buckle down, get your work done—okay?

JEAN   Yes, P'pa.

Silence… then BENOÎT picks up the square of Plexiglas.

BENOÎT   What name you choose for your building?

JEAN   Haven't thought of one yet.

BENOÎT   How 'bout La Belle Tour Penchée de Jean Fournier— *(hands the Plexiglas square to JEAN)* You can put the beautiful leaning tower of Jean Fournier on this…

JEAN   Wow. Thanks, P'pa.

KATHLEEN takes some tinsel out and hands the box to BENOÎT.

JEAN stares at the Plexiglas. BENOÎT and KATHLEEN put tinsel on the tree.

BENOÎT   I don't understand how anyone could do that to their children.

KATE   Eh?

BENOÎT   That guy's father... beating his own kids like that.

KATE   You just put the tinsel on and never mind that guy. Those people are permanently out of our lives.

Blackout.

Scene Six

"The women... they're following me."

July 1990.

It's dark. JEAN lays on the couch in his pyjamas. The television is on but the sound is turned down. Light and shadows from the screen flicker across JEAN's sleeping face.

Hovering like a ghost in the background, the structure—without the Plexiglas square—leans only very slightly to one side.

Without opening his eyes JEAN begins to scream... a high-pitched scream that starts softly then builds into a frightened howl, like a tenor going into shock when he hits high C.

After a moment, KATHLEEN enters in her nightgown.

KATE   Jean, Jean—

JEAN   Oh oh oh oh...

KATE   What's the matter?

JEAN wakes up—panicked, frightened.

JEAN	...run down the escalator oh oh oh oh oh run—
KATE	You all right?
JEAN	...RUN!
KATE	Jean... Jean?
JEAN	...oh oh oh oh—
KATE	JEAN.
JEAN	...yeah, yeah... sorry, Ma.
KATE	Scare me half to death. Went into your room and you weren't there.
JEAN	Came out to watch TV.
KATE	Another nightmare?

He nods his head heavily, yes.

JEAN	...oh, oh, oh...
KATE	Shhhh. I'll make you some hot chocolate.
JEAN	It's too hot, Ma.
KATE	Ice water.
JEAN	No.
KATE	I made special ice water with pieces of lemon in it.
JEAN	Oh, my head feels... loaded.

BENOÎT saunters into the room wearing only pyjama bottoms.

BENOÎT	What's all the commotion?
KATE	Nightmares again.
BENOÎT	*(to JEAN)* You okay now, Jean?
JEAN	Yeah P'pa.
BENOÎT	You sure?
JEAN	My head aches...
BENOÎT	Hotter than hell in here.

KATE   All the windows are open. Tomorrow's gonna be even hotter.

BENOÎT   If Nelson's would install friggin' air conditioning least I'd be cool during the day. Living in their air-conditioned mansions with maids and martinis and friggin' limousines but oh no they can't find the cash to put in AC—management says the fans give cool ventilation year around—cool, for sure, when it's 20 below—*calisse*.

KATE   You want some ice water?

BENOÎT   Eh?

KATE   I made ice water with pieces of lemon floating in it—it'll cool you off.

BENOÎT   Okay.

She exits into the kitchen... a light goes on.

They got air conditioning over at Provigo?

JEAN   Yeah.

BENOÎT   Lucky you. I'm gonna lose five pounds just from sweating.

JEAN   You can have the little fan in my room.

BENOÎT   Ah, that's hardly a breath of air.

JEAN   Go ahead—take it. I'm not that hot.

BENOÎT   When I got polio, kids they teased me 'cause I couldn't do sports. Had bad dreams, too—dreamt I was crippled, couldn't run from people chasing me. I hated doing the special exercises—hurt like hell, but the more I did them, the less they hurt.

The kitchen light goes off. KATE enters with a glass of ice water and gives it to BENOÎT.

...time, eh. Time makes things a bit better. You get some sleep now, eh—goodnight.

JEAN   Take the fan from my room, P'pa.

BENOÎT ...keep it. *(indicates his lemon drink)* I got this to cool me off.

> *BENOÎT lumbers out of the room and exits SL.*

KATE Sure you don't want a nice cool glass of ice water—

JEAN Ma, I'm sure.

KATE You gonna watch TV or go back to bed?

JEAN Do you know what I dream about sometimes?

KATE What?

JEAN That no one died.

KATE Eh?

JEAN It's a special dream but it starts the same way—he comes in and says "Everyone stop everything," but everybody ignores him until he fires at the ceiling. At first I think it's a scary joke... then he says "Separate— girls on the left, guys on the right." No one even moves 'til he shouts, and then the guys, we go over to the right side where the door is. He waves the women to the back left corner. Then he says "Okay—guys leave, women stay." There's nine women and about forty-five guys and two professors... so we leave the room and a few of us stand out in the hall... we hear the guy talking and a woman talking then bam bam bam... but in the special dream I... I run back into the classroom and he's standing there, his back to me, I could see the women bunched up against the wall, moaning and... ah... I was so scared 'cause I never open my mouth in class—even when I don't under- stand something I just sit there praying someone else will ask the question but suddenly I hear someone shout STOP. At first I think it's a professor who walked in behind me or a policeman but it's me, I'm shouting at the guy and he swings around and fires and I veer to one side and I say PUT IT DOWN but he just keeps firing so I take a bullet in the leg, another in the side of my head then calculate that the only way to stop the guy is tackle him—he's only about five-foot ten, skinny, maybe a hundred and fifty—so I jump him and his eyes open wide and he runs out of the room and I'm screaming to the guys out in the hall to stop him... then... then I start sprouting extra arms so I scoop up the wounded women until they're all in my arms and I run out and down the corridor, covered in blood, running behind him screaming YOU FUCKING COCK SUCKING—

KATE   Jean—

JEAN   MURDERING FUCK PIG SAVAGE—

KATE   Jean, stop it—

JEAN   I don't know where all these extra arms are coming from, Ma, but I keep scooping up women , lifting them, holding onto them for dear life until I can hardly move and I'm drowning in their blood but I stagger outside and get them to the ambulances in time and no one died, Ma... then I wake up.

KATE   ...*mon petit* Jean...

JEAN   That's what I most hate, Ma.

KATE   What?

JEAN   That he was so angry and I was so afraid... I was a tiny frightened insect scurrying down the escalator—someone should squish me.

KATE   Shhhh—don't say that.

JEAN   Squish me, Ma. Break my spine.

KATE   You did what you could, Jean.

JEAN   I didn't do anything—nothing.

KATE   You phoned 9-1-1.

JEAN   Yeah, *after* I ran out of the classroom and *before* I ran out of the building.

KATE   Everyone else ran!

JEAN   That doesn't make it okay!

KATE   It's not okay but what else you gonna do when
       a crazy's running around with a gun shooting people.
       This guy I heard on TV he said ordinary people aren't
       expected to be heroes in those situations. He said
       okay—people panic, they freeze or they run—if you
       froze you prob'ly would have been killed.

JEAN   That's not the point, Ma—point is no one tried to stop
       him.

KATE   The point is you're still alive.

JEAN   It's not enough to still be alive!

KATE   Yes, it is—you can build buildings and hospitals and
       churches—

JEAN   Those women will never build anything!

       Silence.

       Ma.

KATE   What?

JEAN   Maybe I'm dead, too.

KATE   Eh?

JEAN   Maybe I didn't get to the ambulance in time.

KATE   Don't talk crazy.

JEAN   He killed me, Ma.

KATE   Your father quit smoking New Year's and it's still hard
       for him. He sweats, gets up at night crying, he suffers
       at work 'cause the guys they tease him but he takes it
       one day at a time—that's what you have to do.

JEAN   Please could I take karate lessons?

KATE   We don't have the money for stuff like that—don't
       keep asking me.

JEAN   I'll save up my allowance plus use some money from
       work.

KATE   That money you earn at Provigo is for next year's tuition.

JEAN   But I have to be prepared for when it happens again.

KATE   It'll never happen again.

JEAN   I want it to happen again—and when Marc fuckin' Lépine comes bursting into class I'll have muscles and reflexes... and guts. I left those women once but next time I'll stand and fight—girls on one side, mice on the other, girls on one side, chickens on the other, you monsters get on that side and stay absolutely still or I'll yank your fucking faces off—

KATE   Calm down or my heart's gonna start beating too fast.

JEAN   I ran out of the classroom and I ran and ran then I missed the bus and figured that was a sign for me to turn back but I was cold so I got on the Metro at Côte-Sainte-Catherine and decided I'd just go one stop then get off at Plamondon and go back to the school but I went right past Plamondon past Namur past De La Savane and when I got off at Du Collège I automatically started walking down Ste. Croix. I kept telling myself to turn around turn around turn around but I was shaking so I ran along Rue Hodge then turned onto Rue Petit and... *(begins to weep)* ...I left them all to die.

She puts her arms around him and he snuggles into her breast. She begins to hum a lullaby. Her voice is thin and off pitch but she hums with a determination to soothe her son's turmoil.

Ma?

KATE   Yes, Jean.

JEAN   They're following me.

KATE   Who?

JEAN   The women. They're following me.

Blackout.

Scene Seven

"...the fucking chickens on that side..."

April 1990.

Morning sun leaks through the sheers pulled across the window. JEAN comes into the living room from the kitchen. He wears pressed black pants, a white shirt and a tie, and knitted slippers on his feet.

Preoccupied, he goes over to the structure and examines some of his notes. The structure is straight. The base of it is only partially covered with an outer layer and therefore the sparse skeletal beauty of the structure can be glimpsed for the first time.

KATE   *(off)* Come finish your breakfast.

> *JEAN concentrates on a notebook that is full of calculations and diagrams.*

         (off) Sausages are your favourite, eh? Jean?

JEAN   I'm not in the mood for sausages.

KATE   *(off)* Why not?

BENOÎT   *(off)* Leave him be.

KATE   *(off)* What am I gonna do—throw them in the garbage? Millions of poor people around the world starving to death—they'd kill for a sausage.

BENOÎT   *(off)* I'll eat them.

KATE   *(off)* Jean?

JEAN   Put one in my lunch pail tomorrow.

KATE   *(off)* You can't carry sausages around like that... what's that disease you catch from meat that doesn't get refrigerated.

BENOÎT   *(off)* Can't get salmonella from cooked sausage.

> *KATE enters wearing a full apron over her good Sunday clothes.*

KATE   I got stew for supper... you wanna know how much stew beef costs?

JEAN   Ma, don't—

KATE   You gonna be in the mood for stew or not?

JEAN   Ma, I have to work on this.

KATE   I thought it's not due 'til next year.

JEAN   Yeah, but it'll take months to do all the calculations—everything has to equal zero.

KATE   You should be studying for your finals—when's the first one?

JEAN   Wednesday morning.

KATE   Should be studying every spare minute, Jean.

JEAN   I'll study, okay—tonight, tomorrow, Tuesday—I'll study—don't keep bugging me.

KATE   I'm asking you a question—

JEAN   Right now I feel like working on my design project because I feel like working on my design project, so quit bugging me.

KATE   I'm not bugging you, I just—

JEAN   That's all you ever do—second I come through the door—Jean do this, do that, always hovering 'round me like I'm a baby—I'm not a fucking baby—

KATE   Don't you ever swear at me—

She raises her hand to swat him, but he grabs her hand.

JEAN   I mean it, Ma—lay off.

KATE   Don't you talk to me like—I'm your mother!

BENOÎT enters wearing good pants, a clean pressed shirt and a tie.

BENOÎT   *(to KATE)* Go do the dishes.

KATE   He said the F word!

BENOÎT   Kathleen—

KATE   What—I'm just trying to get it through his thick skull that—

BENOÎT   Get back in the kitchen and shut your mouth for a change!

KATE exits SR. Sounds are heard as she slams a cupboard door to register her anger then bangs something down on the counter.

Not used to losing his temper, BENOÎT tries to act casual, but he's not a casual man. He peeks out through the sheers.

Boy oh boy oh boy... gonna be a nice spring day. We'll go for a drive after Mass, eh?

JEAN   Yeah, maybe.

BENOÎT   Anywhere special you wanna go?

JEAN   No.

BENOÎT   I'll let you drive. We can drive over and see how construction's going on the Biodome. I hear they're gonna squeeze Antarctica right inside the building— snow and everything, maybe a jungle or two. Gonna be something to see, eh?

JEAN   I'm trying to concentrate.

BENOÎT   Come and sit down.

JEAN   P'pa—

BENOÎT   Sit down.

JEAN sits down. BENOÎT carefully pulls up the knees of his pants before he sits down on the couch beside JEAN.

Things pretty rough, eh?

JEAN   Yeah.

BENOÎT   When I was 'bout ten I went ice fishing over in Sainte Catherine. It was a big deal 'cause we didn't have a car so our neighbours they'd invite P'pa and me to go with them once in a while. We'd catch trout, maybe perch. That day we walked out onto the bay. There was lot of people fishing, lot of holes, big commotion— fish aren't stupid, they sense things getting busy they take off. P'pa asked me to walk further out and check the ice so he could fish away from the crowd. I go out a bit further then start taking baby steps, little bit further, little bit further... see if any cracks appear. It's 'bout ten below, ice is pretty solid so I tell P'pa to come over to where I'm standing. Okay, he pulls up his line, grabs our packsack and starts to walk over to me... he's laughing about something a guy behind him says—P'pa, he was a pretty happy guy in public so he's walking, coming closer to me then suddenly the ice cracks open right under him—his mouth pops open. Shoulda seen him trying to crawl out of the freezing water—grabbing on to the edge of the ice then slipping under again, slopping around like a big seal, snapping, screaming. Everyone come running and formed a human chain to pull him out. He was near froze and madder than a wild pig—boy oh boy oh boy he cursed me out. I blamed myself mostly— but I was just a little kid—weighed maybe seventy pounds, P'pa he was 280 at least—

JEAN   Can't exactly compare falling through ice to what happened.

BENOÎT   No, no—no comparison for sure not, but all I'm saying is you can blame yourself forever, or else understand it's not all your fault and let the thing go.

JEAN   I'm reading a book about karate. Did you know that karate's not really about fighting—it's about self-perfection?

BENOÎT   Well, I don't know much about that.

JEAN   It's about preparing your mind for battle.

BENOÎT   What battle?

JEAN   A battle—any battle.

BENOÎT   You got a battle going on?

JEAN   …sort of.

BENOÎT   Maybe you should talk to someone—some of those grief people.

JEAN   Counsellors.

BENOÎT   Yeah—they still at the school?

>   *JEAN nods, yes.*

You talk to them?

JEAN   I don't like talking to strangers.

BENOÎT   Wanna talk to Father Bonnière?

JEAN   It's not like I think about this stuff every day.

BENOÎT   Father Bonnière baptized you. Go talk to him.

JEAN   Maybe.

BENOÎT   What about your friends? You ever talk to them?

JEAN   No one talks about it much.

BENOÎT   Before Christmas, Ma mentioned a girl you were seeing. Can you talk to her?

>   *A long, uncomfortable silence… then JEAN gets up and goes back to his structure. BENOÎT is not sure what to say or do.*

Whatcha going to call your building?

JEAN   You mean like a name?

BENOÎT   Yeah—like the Sun Life Building.

JEAN   Don't know yet.

BENOÎT   Kinda skinny. A big wind come along might blow it right over.

JEAN   These are built to withstand high winds—even earthquakes.

BENOÎT   How do you do that?

JEAN
Easy. First I calculate the dead load—which is the weight of the structure; then I calculate the live load—which are objects like people and furniture. The structure has to withstand all the loads that will be placed upon it or it will fail—fall apart.

BENOÎT
But how do you know how much weight the building's gonna handle in the future?

JEAN
You work with maximum calculations, and as long as design loads are not exceeded the structure should spring back when the load is lifted, or hold steady indefinitely. Remember me telling you about resisting deformation?

BENOÎT
...yep.

JEAN
Columns and beams clustered in the middle create stiffness—you understand that?

BENOÎT
...yep, pretty much. Absolutely.

JEAN
Look at this, P'pa.

JEAN opens his notebook and shows his father the diagrams.

That shear core around the elevator shaft helps the structure resist rocking forces.

BENOÎT
Okay, but it's gotta have some give else it'll crack in half.

JEAN
Yeah, but it's a perfect balance between resistance and give. Our professor told us about the Hyatt Regency collapse in 1981. A crowd of people in the Kansas City Hyatt hotel lobby were watching and dancing to a swing band... lobby was an atrium with elevated walkways suspended across it. People were dancing on the walkways so it was undulating a little... suddenly everything collapsed—114 people killed, 200 injured. That's what happens when you fail to perform calculations to determine the load capacity of your design. So along with load calculations, I have to take into consideration the temperature, vibrations, and the materials used.

BENOÎT   Boy oh boy, you gotta be smart to figure all that stuff out, eh?

JEAN   Last week I only got 79 on my heat transfer presentation.

BENOÎT   That's pretty good.

JEAN   No it's not.

BENOÎT   For sure you'll get a hundred on this.

JEAN   There's a lot of paperwork left to do but we were given a half-year extension 'cause of what happened—it's not due until the first of December so I'll finish it over the summer. I just wish my hands worked faster. When I close my eyes I can see the whole building inside my head.

BENOÎT   Wow, that's something.

JEAN   I can swivel the building around and feel all its dimensions—I can even change them. Just like this, eh—a thought and poof! I see inside and outside at the same time, as if I'm flying through the structure, creating it as I go. I bet I could build a whole city in my head.

> *KATE, who has been peeking around the corner, enters room* sans *apron.*

KATE   How's he doing?

BENOÎT   Fine. I'm just telling him he shouldn't swear in front you.

KATE   Shouldn't swear, period.

JEAN   Sorry, Ma.

BENOÎT   *(to JEAN)* Okay, go get ready.

JEAN   Don't feel like going to Mass this morning.

BENOÎT   Eh?

KATE   Now you listen to—

BENOÎT   Kathleen—leave him be—

KATE   It's Palm Sunday!

BENOÎT Won't hurt just once.

KATE   He can't miss Palm Sunday—*(to JEAN)* what on earth is wrong with you?

JEAN   I just feel that I... I want to stay home.

KATE   First sausages, now Mass—what next? Not gonna be in the mood to go to school? *(to BENOÎT)* Know who I blame—I blame that guy and that guy's mother. You gotta ask what the heck kind of mother allows her son to run around with a big gun and a bag of bullets, eh?

BENOÎT Just let it go, Kate.

KATE   I hear all kinds of things—most of them true.

BENOÎT You don't know what's true and what's not true.

KATE   Madeleine heard that the killer's real name was Gamil Gharbi and his father was a Muslim from Algeria and he got rejected from the army 'cause he was crazy.

      JEAN covers his ears.

BENOÎT Who—the father?

KATE   No, the crazy killer son. Army wouldn't even take him. I tell you, Benoît, that family shoulda been run outta town on a razor blade—

BENOÎT You calm down—I mean it—enough! God will understand that Jean's had a rough time. C'mon—I hate being late...

      BENOÎT exits SR.

KATE   God might understand but I don't. You're saying the rosary right after supper tonight—two times.

JEAN   Okay.

BENOÎT *(off)* Kate!

KATE   And when we leave, no turning on the TV.

JEAN   No, Ma.

JEAN waits until he hears the back door closing then he performs what he thinks are karate moves and tries to deepen his voice...

...the boys on this side, the girls on that side, lambs sleep on this side, wolves on that side, cows on this side, bulls on that side, chickens on this side... the chickens... the fucking chickens... on this side, the fucking chickens on that side...

...his movements are unformed. Awkward. Desperate.

Blackout.

Scene Eight

"...you're safe, Jean, you're safe."

December 1989.

The living room is dark. Streetlights and a hint of cold snowy weather leak through the sheers.

The back door is heard opening and closing... then the sound of stamping boots knocking off snow. After a moment, KATHLEEN enters and turns on the lights. She wears her old winter coat, a pair of knitted slippers on her feet, and carries a very large Hudson's Bay bag that she gently lays on the couch... then she exits SR.

In the corner stands the first incarnation of JEAN's design project, a meticulous model, an austere miniature skeletal frame for a tall, ultra modern building.

After a moment, KATHLEEN re-enters sans her coat. She hums a Christmas carol as she closes the drapes, turns on the lamp then exits SL. Everything in the living room is neat and polished. She re-enters carrying a newspaper. She drops the paper on the Lazee-Boy then exits SR. From the kitchen can be heard the sound of cupboard doors opening and pots and dishes being taken out. The back door is heard opening and closing again, then the sound of stamping boots.

BENOÎT   *(off)* *Bonjour, ma belle.*

KATE   *(off)* You remember to bring back your spare lunch pail? I had to pack Jean's lunch in a paper bag this morning.

BENOÎT   *(off)* Tomorrow for sure, *ma belle.*

KATE   *(off)* For sure, *ma belle*, for sure.

> *BENOÎT enters the living room from SR, his face still red from the cold outside, knitted slippers on his feet. He notices the bag.*

BENOÎT   Whatcha do? Buy out the store?

> *KATHLEEN enters wearing an apron.*

KATE   Got it on sale, eh.

> *KATHLEEN reaches into the bag and pulls out a man's red winter parka.*

They come in black and navy but I like the red. Simone and I went over to the Bay at lunch. She got tights and sweaters for her girls. Usually don't get these big sales 'til after Christmas. *(holds up the parka)* Think he'll like it?

BENOÎT   *C'est bien beau, c'est sharp.*

KATE   Try it on.

> *He does so.*

Put up the hood.

> *He pulls the hood over his head.*

Looks good, eh?

BENOÎT   Yep. Nice and warm, too.

KATE   Sure he'll like it?

BENOÎT   Yep. Santa gonna bring me one like this for Christmas, too?

> *KATE takes the parka off BENOÎT.*

KATE   Keep dreaming.

BENOÎT   If I'm good, eh?

KATE   Good, bad, doesn't matter—we can't afford a new parka for you 'til next year.

BENOÎT   ...ahhh.

KATE   Don't know where I'm gonna get big enough wrapping paper to cover it.

BENOÎT   Put in a box—makes it smaller.

KATE   The Bay didn't have boxes big enough.

BENOÎT   Might be an empty one in the basement somewhere.

KATE   Go down and see.

>   *BENOÎT stares at the jacket.*

BENOÎT   Maybe it's too... too young.

KATE   Size 40 isn't young. Besides I can't return it—final sale.

BENOÎT   It's the hood... like little kiddies wear.

KATE   It's removable. See, Jean can just unzip it like so...

>   *She unzips the hood.*

BENOÎT   Looks better like that—more manly.

KATE   Too cold to be running around without a hood.

BENOÎT   Better put it away case he walks in.

KATE   I'll hide it in our bedroom—run down and get that box.

BENOÎT   He got a new parka two years ago—how come he's getting another one?

KATE   Boys grow, Benoît.

>   *He exits SR.*

>   *(calls after him)* Bring up the decorations while you're down there!

>   *She zips the hood back on, lays the parka on the couch and folds it up gently as if folding a mink coat.*

>   *BENOÎT re-enters carrying an empty box.*

BENOÎT   I'll get the decorations tomorrow.

KATE   Tomorrow after work we're going with Madeleine to get the tree. Do it now.

BENOÎT   After supper.

He exits SR. She begins putting the folded parka into the box.

KATE   She went to Bernard's this morning and reserved a pine for us. Saturday we'll decorate. Jean can help.

BENOÎT re-enters with a bottle of beer.

BENOÎT   Last year's was too big, too tall. Angel scraped the ceiling.

KATE   She reserved a medium size this time.

BENOÎT   Her medium is everyone else's extra-extra large—even her eyes are fat.

KATE   So she's plump—no need to insult my sister.

BENOÎT picks up the newspaper and sits down on the Lazee-Boy.

BENOÎT   C'mon, plump—she's 350 pounds.

KATE   So she's overweight—what's it to you?

BENOÎT   *(lights a cigarette)* All I'm saying she measures things according to her own size.

KATE   Does she tease you about your limp?

BENOÎT   No one notices it—you need a magnifying glass to notice it.

KATE   How many smokes you had today already?

BENOÎT   'Bout a pack.

KATE   What did Doctor Picard tell you?

BENOÎT   I'm smoking more 'cause in three weeks I'm quitting— five after twelve a.m. first of January 1990—starting the decade brand new.

KATE   It's about time—now help me move his model into the other corner—

BENOÎT   Don't touch it! It's a very delicate thing.

KATE   I know—but we gotta move it into the other corner so we can put the tree there.

BENOÎT   Put the tree in that corner for a change.

KATE   Then people won't be able to see the tree lights from outside.

BENOÎT   Why do they always gotta see the lights from outside?

KATE   It makes the house look inviting.

BENOÎT   Why? No one's coming over 'cept Madeleine and her kids.

KATE   Who knows? Maybe Jean might bring some friends over on Boxing Day for a little glass of cheer and I'll make hot turkey sandwiches for supper.

BENOÎT   When has Jean ever invited anyone for supper? Eh? He's never invited anyone here since what—grade three—when that little girl came over from next door.

KATE   This Christmas he might invite his friends over.

              She takes the packed box and exits SL.

BENOÎT   You and your fantasies—Jean's gonna bring home friends, maybe girlfriends, maybe he'll bring home a small family of dalmatians. He's not gonna bring anyone home 'til he lets go the apron strings and he's not gonna let go 'til you cut them.

              KATHLEEN enters.

KATE   Don't talk stupid.

BENOÎT   He's nearly 22.

KATE   So what.

BENOÎT   So what, so what. Let him live.

              KATE looks out the window.

KATE He's late.

BENOÎT See, that's exactly what I mean. He's twenty minutes late and you're hopping around like a jackrabbit.

KATE He's probably staying after class... talking with friends. He mentioned a girl.

BENOÎT ...he did? When?

KATE Last week. He didn't say her name, just said there was a girl in his class he admired. He said she was pretty and smart and I said, "Guess she's pretty smart," and he chuckled.

BENOÎT That's a good sign.

KATE I got my fingers crossed.

KATE exits SR.

BENOÎT What's for supper?

KATE (*off*) Pork chops.

BENOÎT Oh, boy.

BENOÎT turns on the television...

T.V. ...(*sounds of sirens punctuate as a male reporter speaks*) "...there's pandemonium outside the building as ambulances line up outside the École Polytechnique to take away the injured. There is no official figure available yet but police estimate there may be more than twelve people dead and many others wounded. It appears that someone went on a rampage. Apparently a young man went into a classroom and started shooting."

BENOÎT (*calls*) Kathleen!

T.V. (*male reporter's voice*) "Eyewitness accounts are horrifying. One student reports what he saw..."

KATHLEEN enters holding a carrot and a peeler.

(*young man, in French*) "I went down to the second floor. There were two people on the floor—blood was everywhere." (*male reporter's English translation*) "This

student says, 'I went running down to the second
floor. There were two people lying on the floor—blood
was everywhere.'" *(young man, English, slight accent)*
"The guy walked slowly, he seemed very calm. He
was pointing at... uh... everyone. He shot about uh...
many many times." *(young man, French accent)* "I saw
the guy, the gun was stuck, I thought it was a joke...
so I wait. He went away. I tried to help a girl. The guy
he came back and tried to shoot me because uh...
I was trying to help a girl, so I pretended to be dead."
(young man, English, slight accent) "The guy walked
slowly, he seemed very calm. He was pointing at...
uh... everyone. He shot about uh... about twelve
times." *(male reporter's voice)* "Parents of the
Polytechnique students have begun arriving on the
scene to see what happened to their children."

KATE   *(grabs the phone)* Get me the phone book.

    *He grabs the phone book, but he's so flustered he can't
    turn the pages.*

BENOÎT   Dial Operator.

KATE   *(into the phone)* Put me through to the École
    Polytechnique—University of Montreal.

T.V.   *(male reporter's voice)* "At this moment police still have
    no idea how many have been killed or injured.
    Although it's not confirmed, it appears that the
    shooter, or shooters, may have turned the gun on
    themselves."

KATE   Busy. *(slams down the phone)* Gimme the keys.

BENOÎT   Eh?

KATE   I'm driving up there—gimme the keys.

BENOÎT   I'll drive—

KATE   GIMME THE KEYS?!

BENOÎT   Calm down, you're not friggin' driving anywhere—
    you'll drive into something.

KATE   Go see if he's coming.

BENOÎT   Eh?

KATE   GO OUTSIDE SEE IF HE'S COMING UP THE STREET!

T.V.   *(male reporter's voice)* "Apparently a gunman walked into a classroom of about 60 people with a 22 calibre rifle."

BENOÎT exits SR to get his coat.

KATE   I'll come with you.

T.V.   *(male reporter's voice)* "Witnesses say he separated the men from the women, sent the men outside then started shooting. Police say that after doing that he walked in the hallways and started shooting again. Police are finding victims on three different floors." *(male police representative's voice)* "In French he said— 'You're a bunch of feminists' and he started shooting. I don't know if he separated the men from the women. I don't know that information..."

BENOÎT   *(off)* You stay here in case he phones or the police phone, or—I don't know—

KATE   Don't say that, Benoît... don't you dare say that 'cause if a policeman phones it will be bad news so— *(to the television)* SHUT UP!

She snaps off the television. BENOÎT enters with his boots on and struggling into his jacket.

BENOÎT   Why'd you turn it off?

KATE   Ah, my heart's pounding—feel it... it's gonna blow up.

BENOÎT puts his hand against her chest.

BENOÎT   Take some deep breaths.

She forces herself to breath slowly.

KATE   I'm fine I'm fine—GO.

*He exits SL towards the front door. She takes a deep
breath...*

Dear Jesus don't let Jean be taken don't don't—he's all
I got—he's my baby, don't take my baby away or I'll—
he's young and sweet and goes to Mass every Sunday.
Spare him—I'll make sure he builds you a church,
big, huge—okay maybe not like "Mary, Queen of the
World" but big, something modern. Jean's all for that
modern stuff, he'll build something flashy for you...
oh dear God... *(in BENOÎT's direction)* CAN YOU SEE
HIM?

Silence.

(clasps her hands together and bows her head) "Father,
who dost feed the birds of the air and clothe the lilies
of the valley forsake not the souls of those who trust
in Thee." Don't let him be hurt, spare him spare him
spare—

BENOÎT *(off)* I see him... I SEE HIM!

KATE ...eh?

BENOÎT *(off)* ...he's coming down Cavanagh... he's running!

KATE ...thank you thank you thank you...

*After a long moment, JEAN, completely out of breath,
enters in from SL, an ordinary-looking young man
wearing a shabby brown coat that is too small. He stops
and stares at his mother.*

JEAN ...Ma.

KATE Oh Jean...

BENOÎT enters.

JEAN Something terrible happened.

KATE Jean, *mon petit* Jean...

JEAN Ma...

KATE Thank God you're safe.

KATE throws her arms around her son.

JEAN   Ma…

KATE   …you're safe, Jean, you're safe.

BENOÎT, not used to displaying physical affection, hugs KATHLEEN and JEAN.

Blackout.

fin

photo by Theresa Ho

Born in Rouyn-Noranda, Quebec, Colleen has twice won prizes in the CBC Literary Competition. Her plays include *Beating Heart Cadaver* (nominated for a Governor General's Literary Award) and *The Piper*. Colleen's distinct films include "Putty Worm," "The Feeler," "Shoemaker," "Desire," "War Holes" and "Girl with Dog," and have played in festivals around the world. She lives in Toronto with her husband and son.